HOW DO DRONES WORK?

TECHNOLOGY BOOK FOR KIDS
CHILDREN'S HOW THINGS WORK BOOKS

In this book, we're going to talk about how drones work and how drones are used. So, let's get right to it!

 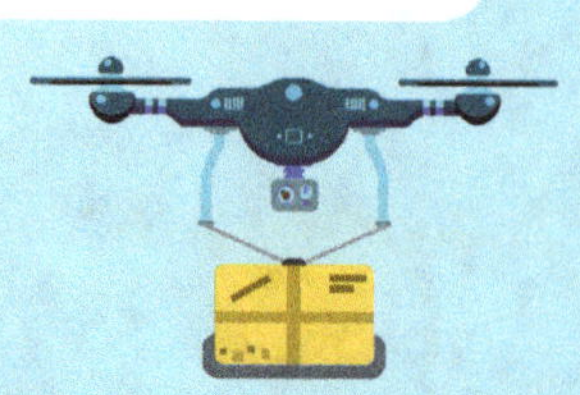

WHAT ARE DRONES?

Drones are unmanned aerial vehicles or UAVs for short. They are operated by remote control. They have many different types of capabilities and have become popular because of their different professional applications. Hobbyists love drones too because they are fun!

They seem to fly effortlessly, but there is really a lot of science behind how drones work. The military uses very large drones, but in this book we're going to talk about drones that are hobby size.

Drones follow the same types of flight principles as other types of remotely controlled vehicles such as model aircraft. However, drones are quadcopters.

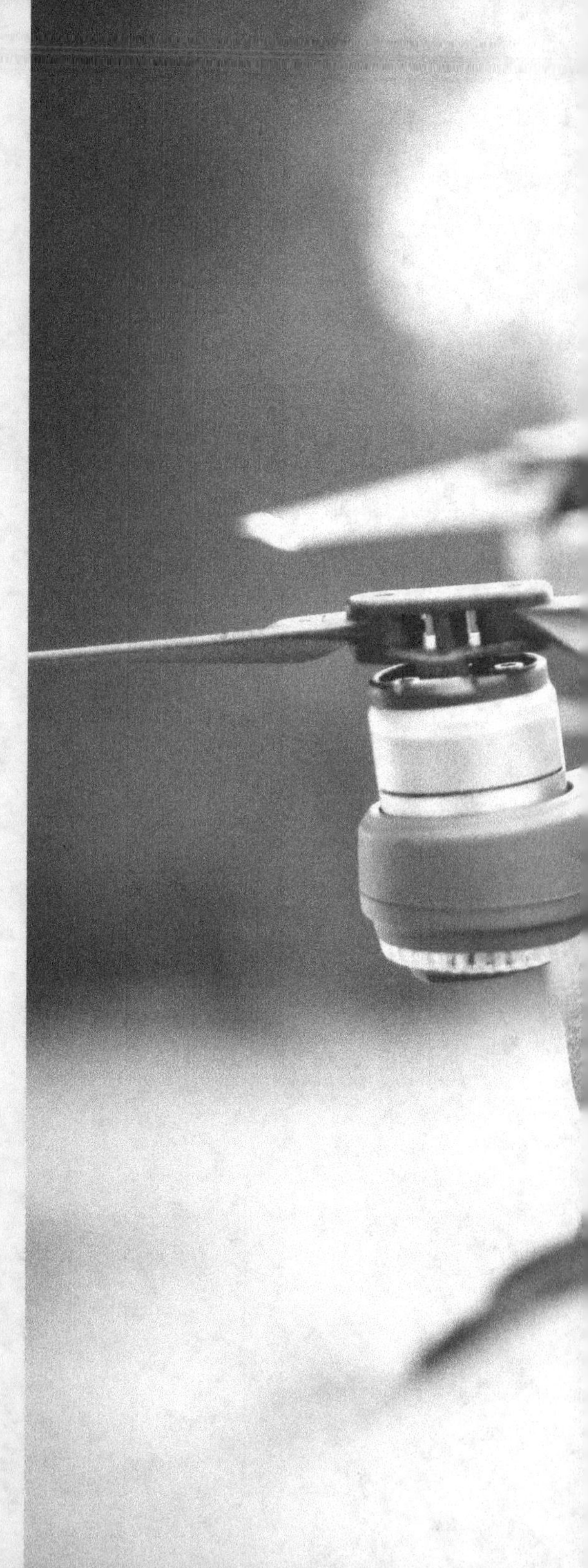

HOW DOES A DRONE CREATE LIFT SO IT CAN FLY?

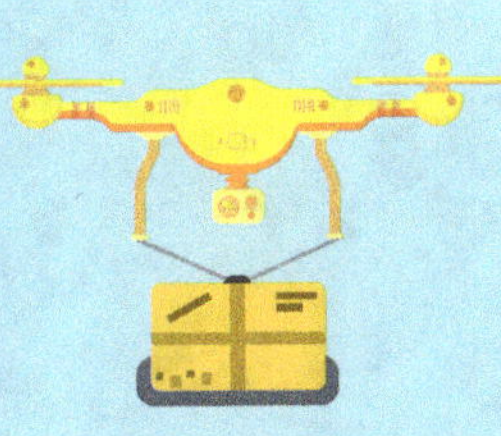

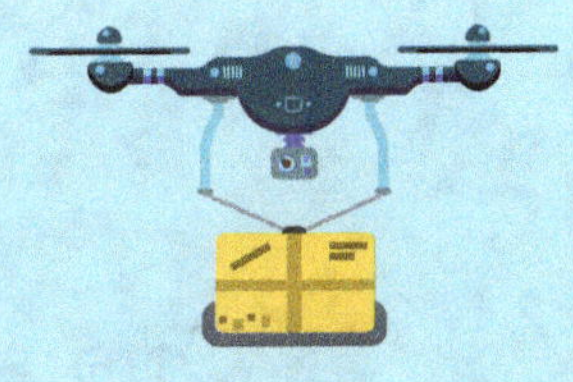

A quadcopter is also called a quadrotor helicopter or quadrotor. It is lifted and propelled in different directions through the use of four rotors as opposed to fixed-wing aircraft like model airplanes. The lift in drones is generated by rotors that are vertically oriented on the craft. In general, they use two sets of identical propellers.

One set of propellers turns clockwise and the other set turns with a counter-clockwise movement. So that the user can maintain control over the vehicle, the speed of each rotor can be individually controlled. By changing the speed of the rotors individually, the total desired thrust can be generated. The center of the thrust can be located both side to side and top to bottom to create the needed turning force, called torque.

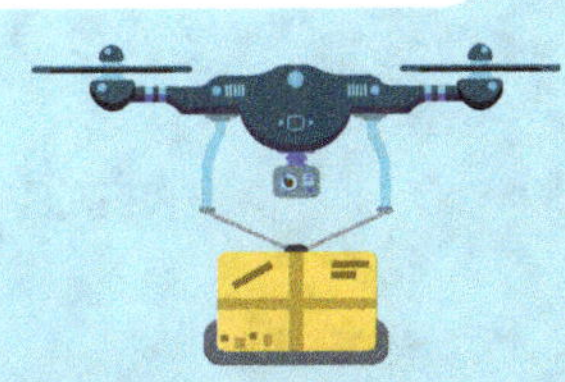

A drone is made from an alloy mainframe that's very lightweight. It has four motors that are run by battery-powered electricity. Each motor has a propeller attached to it. There are speed controllers that are each attached to a motor and are also powered by electricity. There's a mini-computer onboard as well with MEMS, which stands for Micro-Electro-Mechanical-Systems. There are sensors that detect acceleration and there's also a LiPo battery, which is a rechargeable lithium polymer battery.

So, how do all these different components work together to make a drone fly by remote control? Let's look at how the parts work in tandem.

Transmitter

THE TRANSMITTER

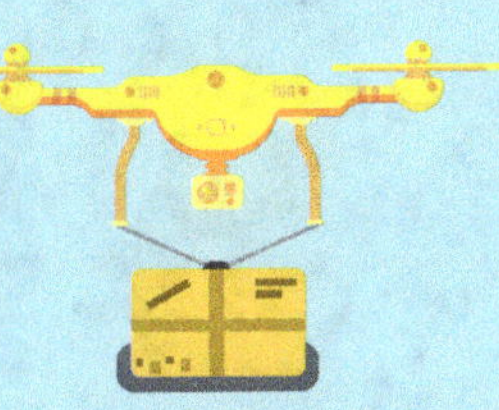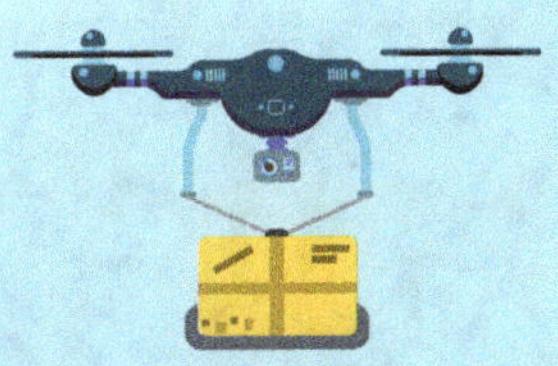

The transmitter is a separate piece of equipment from the drone itself. It can also be an electrical circuit that is found within another electronic device. The job of the transmitter is to allow the user to control the drone remotely from a far distance away. It uses radio signals in the spread spectrum of 2.4 gigahertz. Without the transmitter, you wouldn't be able to control the drone from a distance.

THE RECEIVER

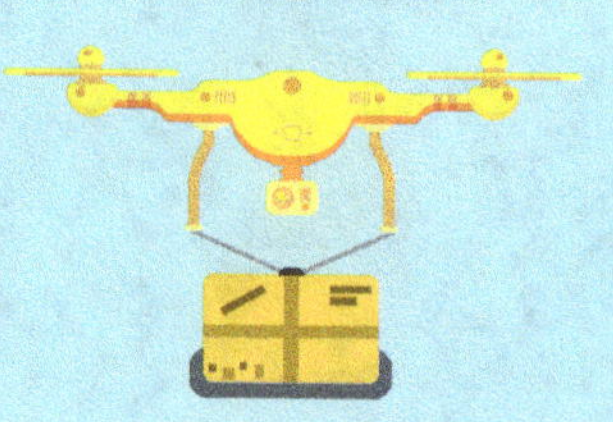
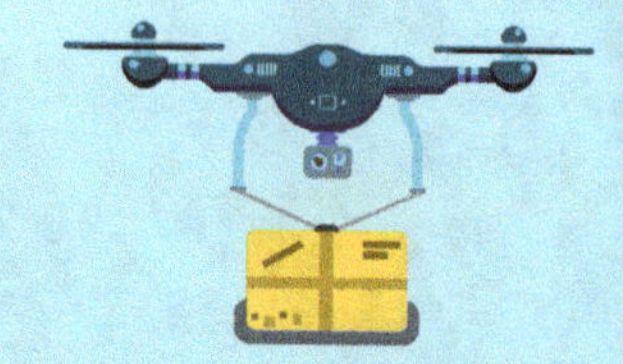

The receiver is another electronic device that is separate from the drone but is needed for the process of operating the drone. It has antennas that are built into it. These antennas pick up the radio signals that have been sent via the transmitter. Those signals are then transformed into pulses of alternating current. The receiver creates information from the current and sends it off to the Flight Control Board of the drone.

CHROMA

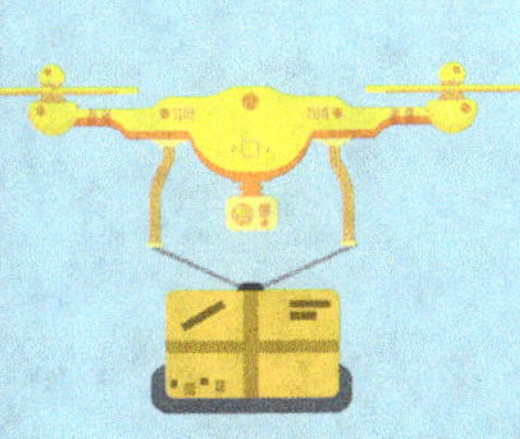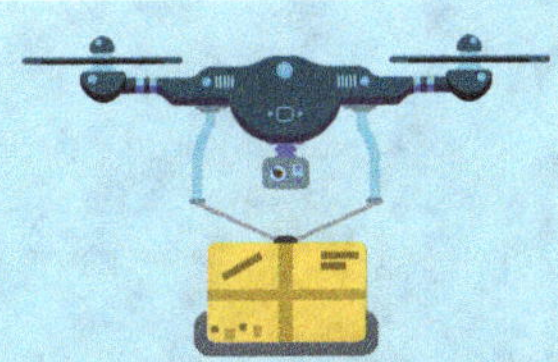

THE FLIGHT CONTROL BOARD

The flight control board is part of the drone. After the transmitter starts sending out radio waves and the LiPo battery is plugged into the drone, the transmitter and the receiver start sending communications to each other. These communications are now sent to the Flight Control Board of the drone.

The job of the onboard sensors is to make sure that the drone remains stable even in very windy conditions. This makes it possible for beginners to operate drones more easily than other types of model aircraft.

MAVIC PRO

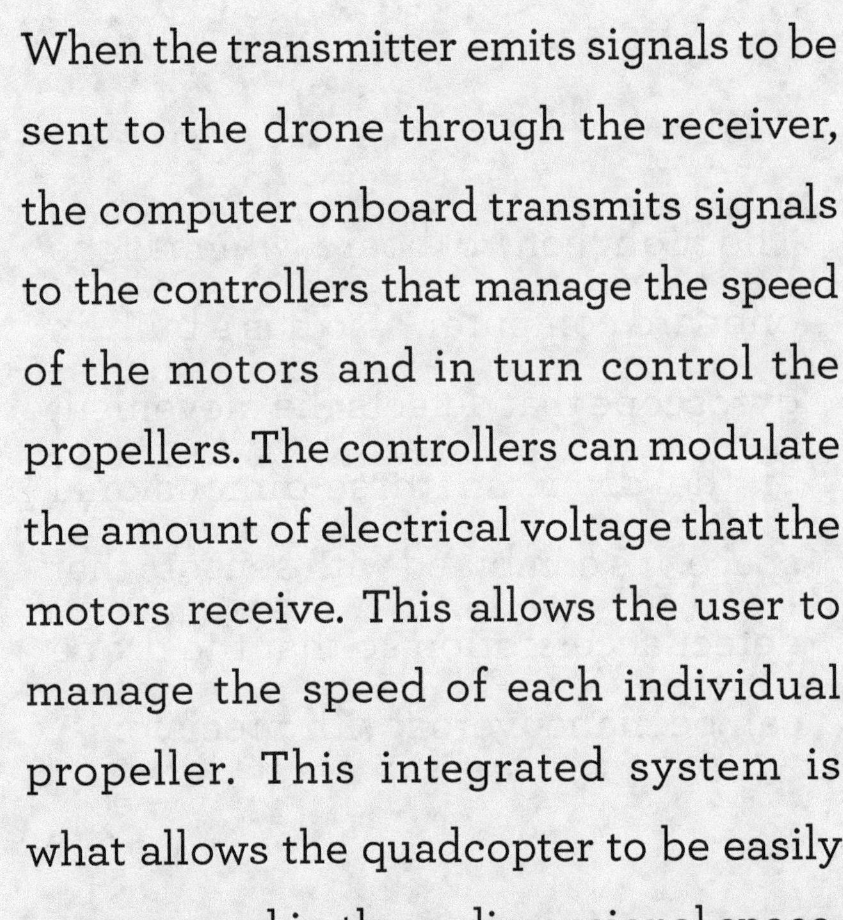

When the transmitter emits signals to be sent to the drone through the receiver, the computer onboard transmits signals to the controllers that manage the speed of the motors and in turn control the propellers. The controllers can modulate the amount of electrical voltage that the motors receive. This allows the user to manage the speed of each individual propeller. This integrated system is what allows the quadcopter to be easily maneuvered in three-dimensional space.

The flight control board, which is the onboard computer, also has a built-in gyroscope that detects the movement of the drone in three-dimensional space. It's combined with sensors that detect acceleration so that the drone can be maneuvered with precision.

RC 5.8G
THE FUTURE OF POSSIBLE

MAVIC PRO

THE BATTERY

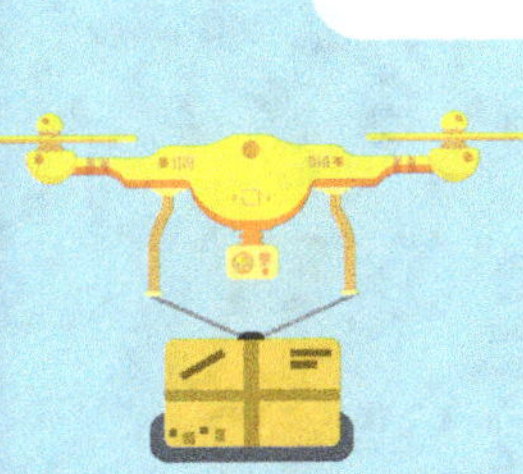

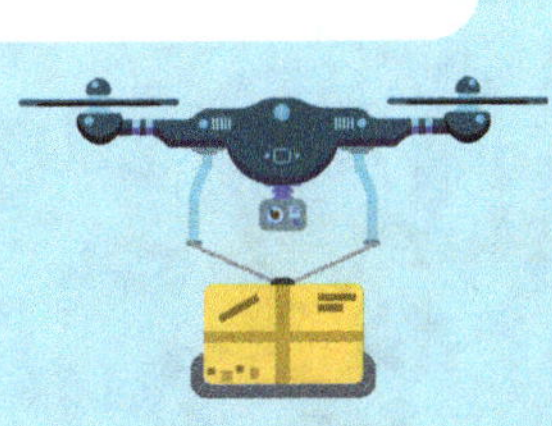

The LiPo battery is rechargeable as well as lightweight. It's a pouch onboard the drone that delivers high rates of electrical energy. It has to provide high enough power to make the brushless electric motors turn to move the propellers.

THE ELECTRONIC SPEED CONTROLLER

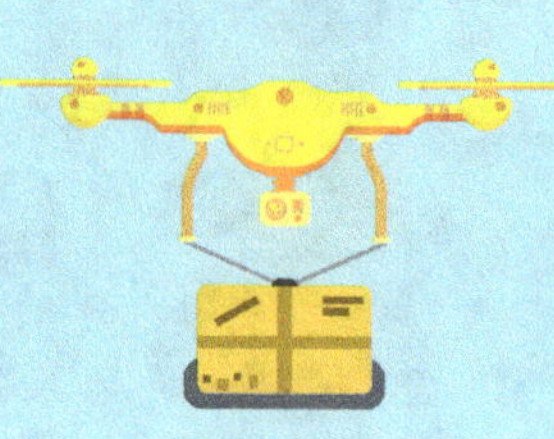
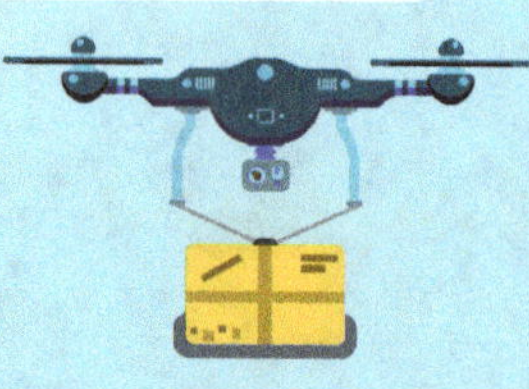

The controller that manages the speed electronically is attached to the battery. It manages the speed of rotation of the electric motor. It does this by adjusting the amperage of the electrical current. This action ensures that the motor is running well and is efficient. The controller has a device built into it that's called a governor. It keeps the rotations per minute or RPM of the motor at a consistent, steady level, no matter what the flight conditions are. It also helps brake the drone if that's necessary.

MAVIC PRO

Q-COPTER

The drone uses a simple electric motor. The user places electricity in the form of battery power into one end and a metal rod called an axle rotates at the opposite end. This action is what makes it possible to drive the propellers on the drone.

In other words, on the outside surface of the motor there are magnets. These magnets are latched onto the inner wall, which is called the rotor. The rotor is the spinning part of the motor. There are also magnets that are permanent inside the static part of the motor, called the stator. As electricity travels through the magnets, it creates a field that is electromagnetic. It alternately attracts then repels the magnets inside the stator. This back-and-forth changing polarity of attraction and repulsion is what keeps the motor operating and spinning.

THE PROPELLER

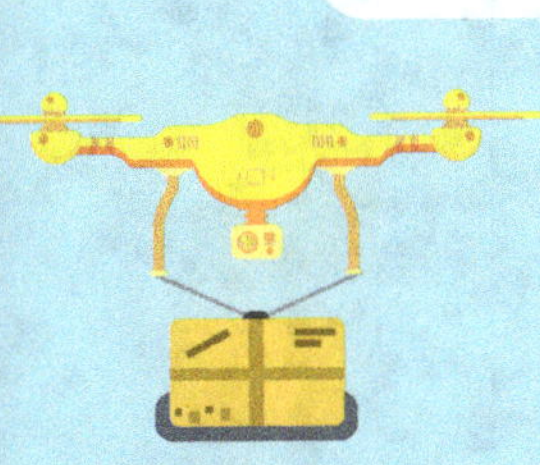
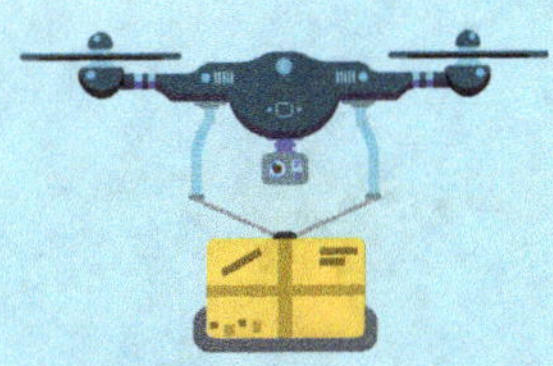

The propellers convert the electric motor's motion into power that lifts the drone skyward. The blades have a special shape that makes the air pressure uneven on the two sides while they are moving. This uneven pressure is what makes the power to lift the drone. Newton's third law of motion and Bernoulli's principle are the underlying physics principles that make it work.

THE CONTROL SURFACE

The onboard computer can control each motor's speed individually. For example, if the two propellers on the drone's right side decrease in rotations per minute, the lifting power will be stronger on the left. As a result, the right side will begin to descend quickly and then the drone will drift right.

The onboard computer will sense the drift and will increase the rotations per minute automatically if the drifting speed reaches the maximum limit. It will position the drone back into a stable position of hovering, even

if the user takes his or her hands off of the controls. This tendency for the onboard computer to correct the motion toward stability is what makes drones easy for beginners to fly.

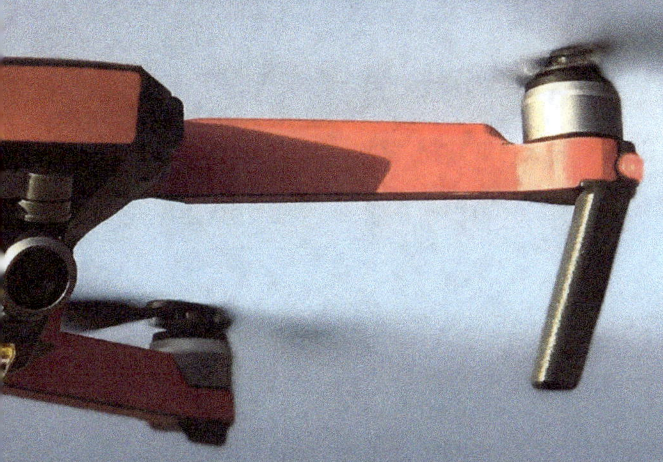

ON-BOARD DIGITAL CAMERA

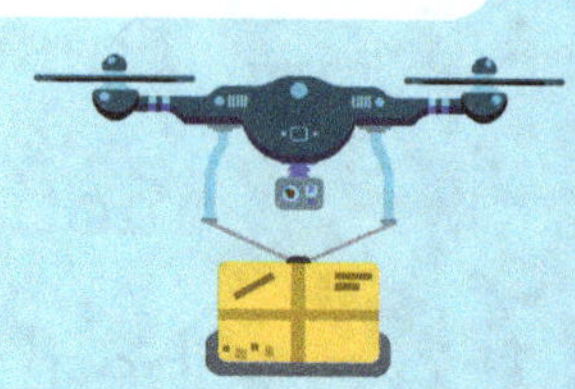

Many types of drones have onboard single-lens digital cameras so you can have the drone take photos while it is in flight!

Drone Camera

WHAT DO DRONES DO?

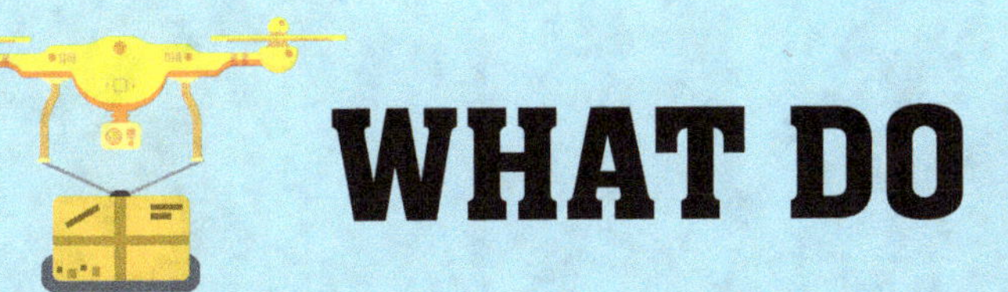

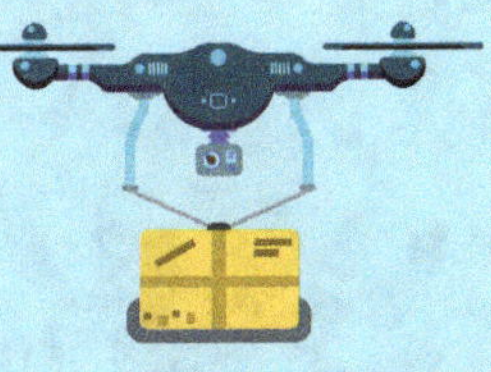

Large drones have been used by the military for a long time for missions that were dangerous for people and also to collect military intelligence. However, it's only been recently that drones have become small enough and agile enough for small commercial uses and for hobbyists. Inventors have been studying how animals fly to improve the technology for drones and there will be many more innovations in the future.

Drones can carry cameras as well as sensors or radio equipment. They can travel places where humans can't easily travel or where it's too dangerous for humans to venture. They can hover like hummingbirds do or swerve around obstacles with the grace of a bat in flight. They can even propel backwards like dragonflies do. They run on clean energy and they're very speedy.

WARNING

Amazon.com and other companies that depend on fast deliveries are investigating the possibility of using drones in the future to deliver goods and food. Solar drones that could stay airborne for over five years are in the works. These types of drones may be able to provide wireless internet to people who live in remote areas.

Drones with cameras on board are already replacing helicopters to gather news and weather reports. Movie and TV producers are using drones to get expansive landscape views for their productions a lot less expensively than hiring pilot-driven aircraft.

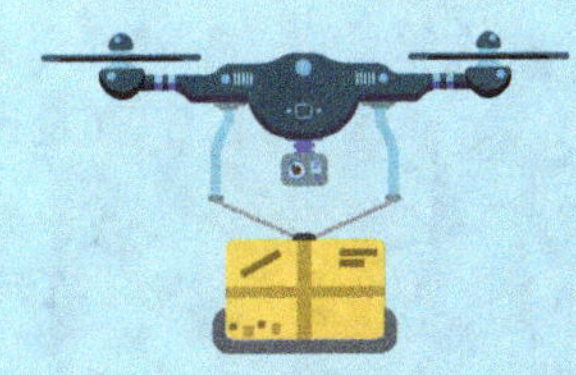

Real estate companies are using drones that can take photographs of properties for sale. Farmers can use them to assess the growth of crops. Hobbyists are having a lot of fun flying drones in their backyards. There are even drones you can fly inside your house!

Of course, with all these drones in the sky people are concerned about privacy. Also, there are safety hazards if people fly drones in areas where they can run into electrical or telephone lines.

SUMMARY

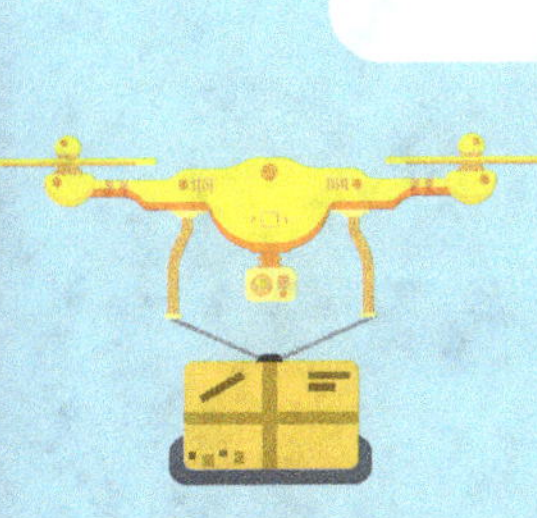

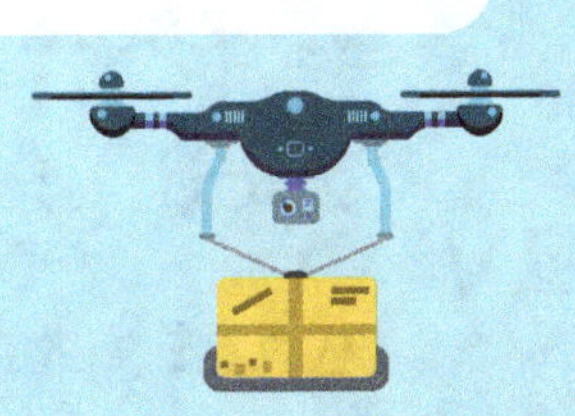

Drones are remote-control quadcopters that use four propellers to create the lift needed to fly. They were originally developed for use in the military but today they are small enough and agile enough for commercial and hobby use. Drones have many different components that work together to make them stable flying vehicles. They're a lot of fun to fly!

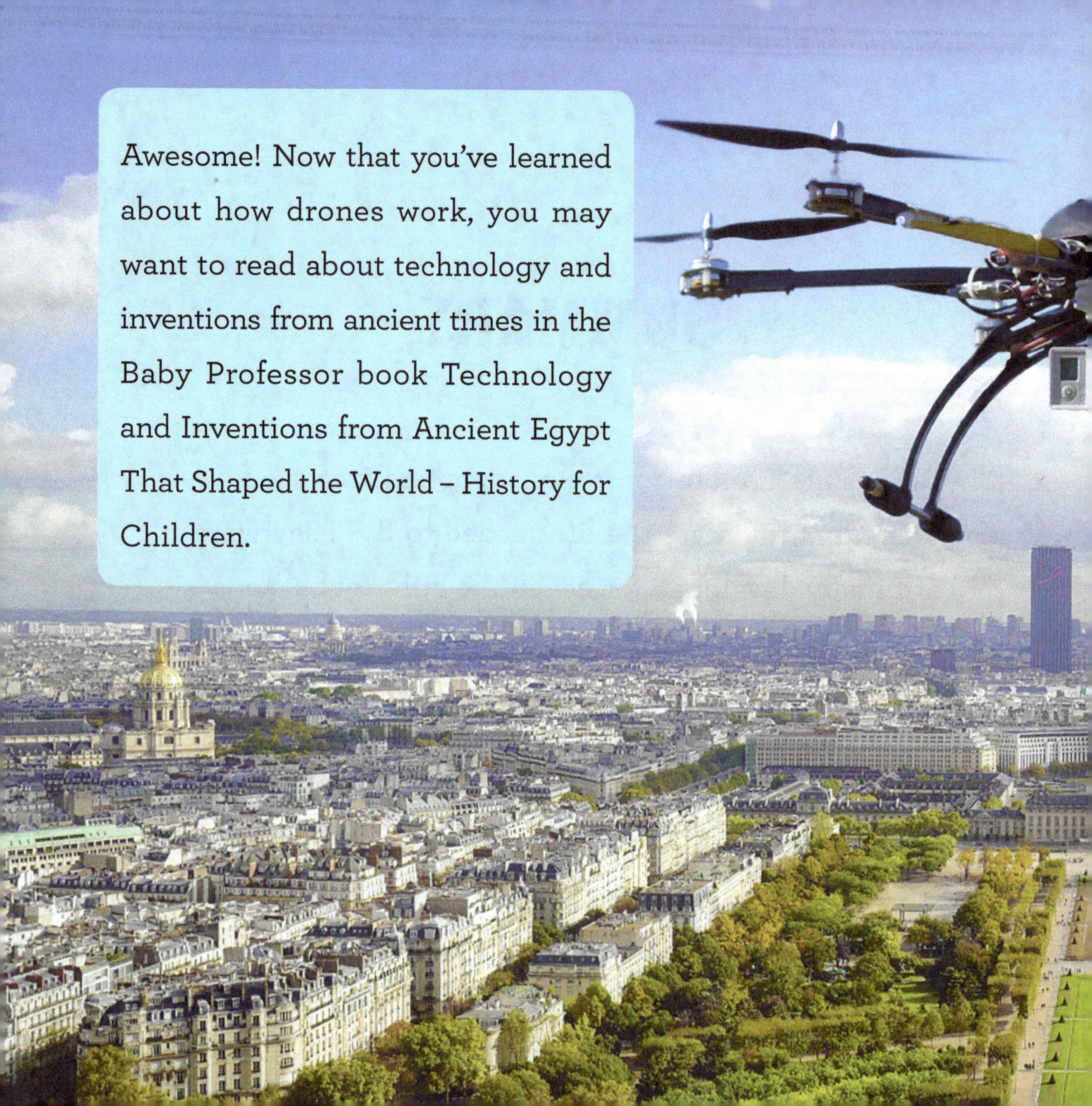
Awesome! Now that you've learned about how drones work, you may want to read about technology and inventions from ancient times in the Baby Professor book Technology and Inventions from Ancient Egypt That Shaped the World – History for Children.

Visit
BABY PROFESSOR
EDUCATION KIDS
www.BabyProfessorBooks.com
to download Free Baby Professor eBooks
and view our catalog of new and exciting
Children's Books